IMAGES OF ENGLAND

BOOTLE
AND ORRELL

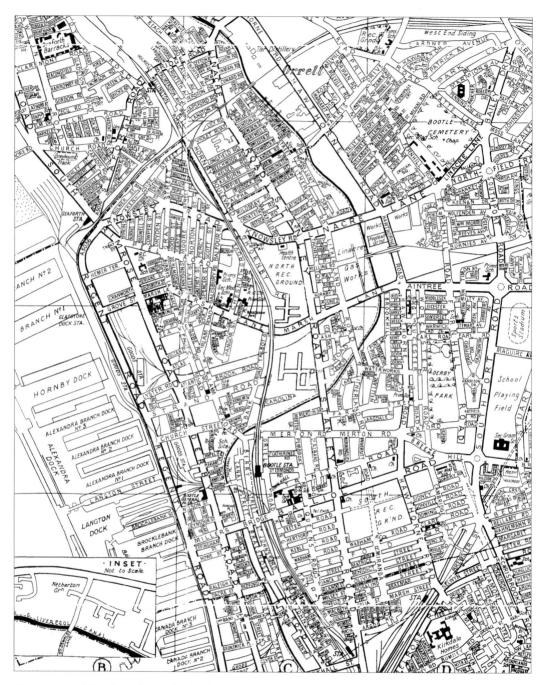

Street map of Bootle and Orrell. This book provides a guided tour around some of the main streets in Bootle and Orrell, which readers can largely follow on foot.

IMAGES OF ENGLAND

BOOTLE AND ORRELL

PETER W. WOOLLEY

TEMPUS

Dedication: This book is dedicated to Sarah and Beth

First published 2004

Tempus Publishing Limited
The Mill, Brimscombe Port,
Stroud, Gloucestershire, GL5 2QG
www.tempus-publishing.com

British Library Cataloguing in Publication Data.
A catalogue record for this book is available from the British Library.

ISBN 0 7524 3360 1

Typesetting and origination by Tempus Publishing Limited.
Printed in Great Britain.

Contents

Acknowledgements

I would like to thank the following persons who have contributed to the production of this book:

Tom Aizlewood, Pastor Brian Astil, Alan Boyle, Paul Bolger, Tom Barber, Bill Bird, Eve Clear, Joan Clough, Pauline Carter, Sid Davis, David Ellison, Steve Hurley, Cath Hankin, Bill Glendenning, Sophie Johnson, Harry Jeffries, Paul Kavanagh, Alice Ford, Philip Mayer, Brenda Montgomery, Tommy McPherson, George Openshaw, Lalla McDermott, Sheila Scott, David White, Harry Wallwork, Mr & Mrs Wanless, Trinity Newspapers, Tom Rooney, Bootle & Orrell History Group, Josie McCabe.

I have been unable to trace the owners of some of the photographs used here, despite extensive enquiries. I am sorry I have not been able to include those people in the acknowledgements but trust that they will be pleased to see their photographs reproduced here.

Bibliography

B.J. Marsh & S. Almond: *The Home Port, Bootle, The Blitz and the Battle of The Atlantic;* 1993; Metropolitan Borough of Sefton
Rob Gell: *Southport & Liverpool Railway Stations*; 1986; Heyday Publishing
Paul Bolger: *Edwardian A-Z Directory of Liverpool & Bootle;* 1999; Stations UK Merseyside
Freddy O'Connor: *A Pub on Every Corner. North Liverpool;* 1998; The Bluecoat Press
Fred Lacy: *Never a Dull Moment;* 1968
Alan Boyle: *Teresa at St Alexanders Bootle*

Introduction

With the opening of Canada Dock in 1859, and the further extension of the docks into Bootle, it was feared that Liverpool's boundaries would gradually stretch and engulf Bootle, thereby swallowing its identity.

A delegation of civic dignitaries travelled to London to campaign against Liverpool taking over Bootle. A Charter of Incorporation for the Borough of Bootle was granted by Queen Victoria in 1869. After being conveyed to Liverpool's Lime Street station by train and then on to the Bootle boundary at Derby Road it was publicly read out by Mr J.W. Cave-Browne-Cave at the Mersey Hotel (now demolished). It was then carried in procession through the streets of Bootle, to St Mary's School on Irlam Road, where it was publicly read out to the populace.

With the construction of the docks Bootle changed dramatically. Gone were the quiet sandy beaches where people would flock to enjoy the fresh air, golden sands, and to watch the sailing ships sailing up and down the River Mersey, travelling to and from distant lands.

The Irish and Welsh flocked to Liverpool and Bootle to find work. Low cost, poor quality houses were built close to the newly-constructed docks in the area around Dacre Street, Dundas Street, Lyons Street, Howe Street, Raleigh Street to Millers Bridge, and between Derby Road and Regent Road. The houses were of back-to-back construction, with cellars. The sanitation was appalling and soon disease and sickness were rife in these terrible living conditions. Cholera, typhoid, typhus and smallpox, to name but a few, caused much suffering and many deaths, and infant mortality was very high. Along with these diseases came social problems; prostitutes, thieves, pick-pockets and every form of low life flocked there for easy pickings. Disturbances and fights were commonplace with women sometimes fighting stripped to the waist.

A notorious double murder in Lyons Street (see p. 37) was dubbed 'The Teapot Murders', because the street bore the name of a well-known brand of tea. The street was renamed Beresford Street in 1878.

The Inspector of Nuisances reported to the Health Committee that on inspecting the cellar of 90 Dundas Street at 1am he found three loose women plying their trade with other men waiting outside for their services. It was a place much frequented by sailors and others, the Committee were told.

If you walk along Derby Road south from Millers Bridge you will come to a cul-de-sac a few yards long. Along with Dundas Street, Howe, Raleigh and Beresford Streets were demolished, and the majority of the area was used for the construction of a ship repairers and engineers.

With the expansion of the docks better quality housing was built on the other side of Derby Road, including St John's Road, Brasenose Road, Bedford Place, Lincoln, Mann, Mathew, William Henry, Kirk and Seaforth Streets, and in the Marsh Lane area. With the trade created by the docks other businesses flourished in the area and Bootle prospered. Transport included trams, trains, and of course, the Liverpool Overhead Railway, which ran until 1956 from Seaforth Sands to Dingle Station.

In this book I have tried to give as varied picture of life in Bootle in the nineteenth, twentieth and twenty-first centuries as possible through the medium of photographs and of old picture postcards. I have not used any photographs from the Second World

War period as they have been used in a superb book, *The Home Port and the Battle of the Atlantic.* The photographs reproduced here have come from family albums, shoe boxes, attics, cellars and wardrobes. Some have not seen the light of day for many years and have never been published before.

The old picture postcards were produced in the 1880s, and were known as Court cards, whereas the postcards that we are familiar with were produced in the early part of the twentieth century. Postcard collecting became a national craze, it was the cheapest form of communication at ½d (a letter would cost 2½d) so many thousands of cards were sent. Postcard publishers photographed every conceivable subject; seaside views, foreign countries, animals, film and variety stars, even nude women. The period prior to the First World War was known as 'the golden age of postcard collecting'. Between 1902 and 1918 millions of postcards were produced annually.

A large number of such cards found their way into family albums as memories of past holidays and portraits of the family. Special albums were manufactured for keeping collections of postcards clean and secure. During the First World War embroidered silk postcards were sent home by the Allied forces. These depicted flags of the Allied nations and were of the envelope type in which a card was inserted with a personal message written on it. After the First World War the postal rate increased to 1d and with the advent of the telephone postcards lost their popularity as a means of communication. Postcard collecting waned and postcard albums and loose postcards were either discarded or stored away. During the Second World War millions of postcards were lost to bomb and fire damage. Some albums found their way into second-hand shops and could be picked up for a few pounds. It is still possible to find the odd album and loose postcards at car-boot sales. Better quality postcards can be found at specialist postcard fairs and at some antique and collectors fairs. As a collecting hobby, postcards are the second most popular after stamps, with collectors from all over the world.

As regards this book I am deeply indebted to local photographers for their contribution to the visual history of Bootle especially William Thomas Wright (W & Co.) who took many photographs of Bootle and surrounding areas. As early as 1896, right up to his death in 1912, he captured changes in Bootle, the docks, shipping, churches, transport, royal visits, portraits, and not forgetting Bootle May Day Demonstrations. Other photographers include Percival Sutcliffe of Hawthorne Road, Terence Ridgeway of Knowsley Road, Harry Dowden of Park Street, plus Cushing, and Foulds & Hibberds, Carbonora, and Jeromes from outside of Bootle.

With the help of these images I will take you on a tour of Bootle, showing streets and buildings, some of which are long gone, and those which have replaced them. I have also included a section on Bootle County Borough Police, complementing the images published in my previous books (*Bootle* and *Bootle: The Second Selection*) as no pictorial record has been published elsewhere.

I hope that this book will evoke lots of memories for the reader, and give as much enjoyment as I have derived during its compilation. If anyone, after reading this book, remembers that they have any postcards or photographs that will be of interest to The Bootle and Orrell History Group, please send or bring them personally to our group. Meetings are held every Monday afternoon, 2pm-4pm, at the Orrell Community Initiatives 'Hub-Nub' building in Linacre Lane, Bootle. All items brought will be copied and returned to you unless you wish to donate them to the History Group.

Peter Woolley
August 2004

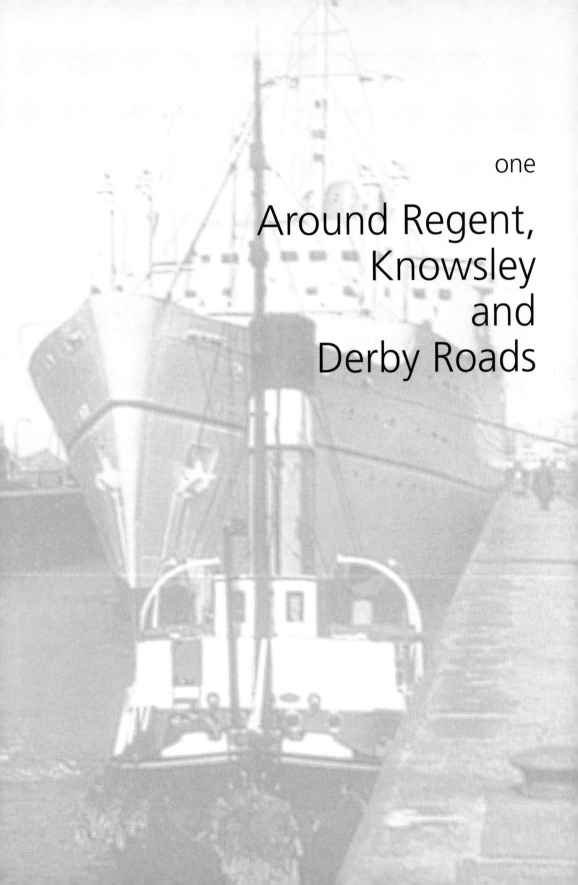

one

Around Regent, Knowsley and Derby Roads

Regent Road, Bootle (Dock Road). Seen from the Liverpool boundary looking into Bootle. At the right is Castle Chambers, which accommodated various companies. Next to it is the Castle Hotel. Adjoining this is Harland & Wolff, ship repairers and engineers. To the far left is the Liverpool Overhead Railway.

Harland & Wolff's premises were built in 1912 and covered a large area that had been the subject of slum clearance, taking in four streets from Derby Road through to Regent Road. The building was badly damaged in the Second World War, and eventually closed down in 1974 due to the decline of the docks and subsequently less ships entering the port. Only the façade remains with the rear yard used for container storage. The Castel Hotel, to its left, is now the Regent Maritime Hotel.

Brocklebank Dock was one of the first docks constructed in Bootle. This postcard was posted in 1902 and shows a mass of ships, masts with only one funnel in view.

The Liverpool Overhead Railway snakes its way towards Seaforth Sands station, passing Alexander Dock station on the left and in the distance Strand Road. The LOR was also known as the dockers umbrella.

Langton Dock on a busy day in 1917. The chimney and clock belong to the hydraulic pumping station which powered the lock gates and bridges. The pump master was Mr Petrie who lived in the pumping station. It was partially destroyed in the First World War and today it is no longer in use.

Alexander Dock goods station, belonging to the London, Midland & Scottish Railway, in 1968. Prominent on the right is the Union Cold Storage. Two grain elevators can be seen in Alexander Dock. The railway line exits under Rimrose Road and on to Fazakerley.

Right: North Wall Lighthouse stood on the River Mersey dock wall between Alexander and Hornby Docks. The white light oscillated and it had a deep resonant sound like a bull, hence its nickname 'The Bootle Bull'. It was demolished during the construction of the Gladstone Docks.

Below: Aerial view of the newly opened Gladstone Docks, which was opened by King George V and Queen Mary. Behind the docks the LOR Seaforth, and part of Bootle can be seen.

North Wall Lighthouse, Liverpool

1913 saw the opening of the first phase of Gladstone Dock. Their Majesties boarded the Mersey Docks & Harbour Companies Tender, *The Galatea,* and sailed up the Mersey to a cavalcade of ships anchored there.

Photographed by William Thomas Wright (W & Co.) of Bootle the cavalcade included the Harrison Line vessel, *Politician*, and the Cunard liner, *Mauretania*. *Galatea* is seen sailing towards *Mauretania* with the royal party ready to board her.

Standing proudly on the deck of *Mauretania* are some of the crew members about to be inspected by King George V, other civic dignitaries and naval personnel. After inspecting the ship the Royal party boarded *Galatea* to sail to the Gladstone Dock.

Bootle jetty, as it was known, is seen here in 1905 with a number of sailing barges plying their trade up and down the Mersey. They carried various cargoes including grain, salt and coal.

Gladstone Dock entrance in 1960. An Empress liner waits in the lock with two tugs from the Alexander Towing Company.

The Cunard liner *Aquitania* was built in 1914 and is seen here from the Liverpool Overhead Railway. She is berthed in Gladstone Dock, prior to her maiden voyage. She was the last Cunarder to have four funnels.

Gladstone Dock gate seen from Fort Road. Just behind the entrance are the police hut, dockers canteen and the largest floating crane in the world 'Mammoth', which towers above the sheds. Above left is the LOR having just left Seaforth Sands station it enters the dock estate.

Fort Road seen from Gladstone Dock gate, looking towards Seaforth Road and Crosby Road. Above is the LOR at Seaforth Sands which had a branch line that could join up with a line of Lancashire and Yorkshire Railway at Litherland Railway Station and could then continue to Aintree (Sefton Arms) as it did during Grand National week.

Happy day trippers paddle and frolic in the clean waters of the River Mersey. They arrived by either tram or overhead railway bringing their bottles of water, lemonade powder, jam butties, and bread and scrape. In the background is the LOR that ran all the way to the Dingle.

An early morning LOR ticket (unused) from Seaforth Sands to Brocklebank Dock. The cost was fourpence halfpenny.

Rimrose Bridge, Rimrose Road, Bootle. On the right is the Winifred Hotel, which at present is closed and boarded up. To the right of the bridge is the sweets and tobacconists shop which served the dockers and other workers for many a year. The bridge carried the LOR branch line.

Along Rimrose Road was St Joan of Arc Catholic school. A large crowd attended the opening ceremony, taken by Archbishop Downey in 1926. Former teachers at the school include comedian Tom O'Connor and broadcaster Peter Maloney.

Throughout the year, as with other churches, St Joan of Arc Catholic church paraded around the parish. This procession was captured in Bibby's Lane. Behind the banner is Miss Mary Billington from No. 61 Peel Road. She was representing St Anthony.

St Leonard's (Church of England) was near to St Joan's and there was always rivalry between the two churches. The Church Lads Brigade are seen marching along Peel Road in 1939. This was the year before the church was destroyed in the bombing in the May blitz in the Second World War.

St Leonard's church championship football team with the cup that they won in June 1939. They are pictured in the grounds of the vicarage of St Leonards.

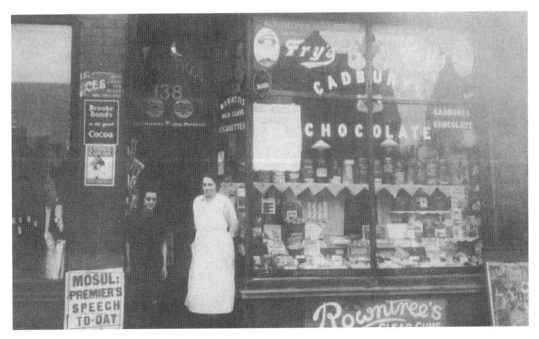

No. 138 Peel Road was the sweets and tobacconists shop belonging to Mrs Margaret Cowl, who lived above the shop. She is standing in the doorway of the shop with a young customer, Miss Alice Barbour, of Shelley Street. The shop and building was destroyed in the blitz. In its place there is a walled garden.

Left: This time-worn photograph is the only known picture in existence to show No. 148 Peel Road, John McPhearsons gentleman's barbers shop. He took over the existing barbers in 1905. It originally had five barbers chairs and was partitioned off from a counter from which sweets and cigarettes and other items were sold. John is standing in the doorway with his uncle who had a barbers in Knowsley Road.

Below: The son of John McPherson, Tom, started working in the shop on Peel Road just after the war, assisting his dad. When his dad died Tom took over the shop. The barbers are only open for a few hours a week now due to falling custom. Tom is seen standing in the doorway holding the broom. In 2005 the business will have been in the family for 100 years and must be the oldest business in Sefton, if not Liverpool.

St Leonard's church 'walk of witness' procession walking along Knowsley Road, near to Dryden Street. George Ash, Pawnbroker, and barbers shop of William Glendenning at 92 Knowsley Road.

This postcard, posted in 1910, shows some of the businesses in Knowsley Road. At No. 112 is Blackledges the bakers, Newey's drapers at No. 110 and No. 108 was the chandlers of Rossiters, No. 106 was Kennards stationers, No. 104 was the chemist and sub-post office. Next door was the Argentinian River Plate Meat Company.

The Gainsboro Cinema in Knowsley Road in 1953. The manager was John Mawdsley. Outside stands a single-decker bus on the 61 route, on its way from Seaforth to Aigburth. Behind it is the Bankhall Mission Hall. On the corner is the bakers of G.H. Parry & Sons Ltd.

Live shows were performed at the 'Gainey' as it was known locally, as well as films. Among the artists posing with manager Stan McCree are Ken Dodd (extreme right), George Martin and Stan Le-Douglas. The others were the 'Langley Variety Mixture'.

The Gainsboro Social Club in the 1980s after it changed from being a cinema into a bingo hall. Gone are the ornate canopy and top of the façade. From this it never really recovered.

This beautiful and well-loved building is pictured during demolition in 2003. Gone is the ornate façade, and only the two entrance arches of the ground floor remain. It is not yet known what this area will now be used for but it is believed that Ryders Garage next door will acquire it for new sales space.

"Gwil" Williams

TENOR AND CARTOONIST

Dear

        This is to remind you that I am again open for engagements during the coming season.

"GWIL" WILLIAMS.

2 SCOTT STREET,
BOOTLE.

An advertising postcard informing variety agents that 'Gwil Williams' tenor and cartoonist is available for bookings. He lived at 2 Scott Street, Bootle.

Joseph Gardner and Sons Ltd timber merchants had been in business since 1748. These premises in Bootle were in Peel Road and were built in 1907. The Bootle side of the business closed in 1948.

Left: A group of children watch as the photographer takes a picture of St James" Catholic church in Chestnut Grove, in 1904. It is known as Bootles' Cathedral and was built in 1886. It contains a valuable and beautiful reredos.

Below: The mission to St James" church took place in September 1925. It was attended, as seen on this postcard, by Father Murphy, Father O'Neil, Father Hulohan, Father Phelan and Monsignor O'Brien.

A MOMENTO OF THE MISSION AT St JAMES, BOOTLE, SEPT. 1925.   T.R.

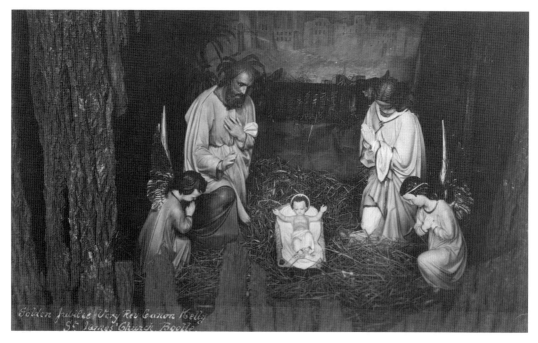

Nativity scene at St James" church in 1906, the jubilee year of Canon Kelly.

This boxing match was an annual event, during Grand National week. Many jockeys, trainers and stable lads attended, and helped to raise money for St James" church. This contest, between John Caldwell (left) and Pat Donaghue, took place in the covered-over swimming baths in March 1927.

Miss Wareham (headmistress) and Miss Polly Wareham (teacher) were sisters, and are shown with some of the pupils in class at Salisbury Road School in 1910. On the back row, second left is Miss Dora Oliver, aged six.

The Salisbury Hotel on the corner of Marsh Lane and Salisbury Road survives and thrives today unlike a lot of pubs round here that have closed down and then mysteriously caught fire!

TRUE PHOTOGRAPH OF
APPARITION WHICH
APPEARED ON WINDOW
AT No. 4, TENNYSON STREET,
BOOTLE.

OUR LADY OF LOURDES
PRAY FOR US!

In the 1940s at No. 4 Tennyson Street, off Marsh Lane, it was reported that an apparition had appeared on the rear ground-floor window. It looked like the figure of the Virgin Mary. This caused an uproar in the area but, though reported in the local press, it did not make the nationals due to the war reports. After a week the apparition disappeared. Some said it was a fake. Others believed it.

TIMBER IMPORTERS

MERCHANTS and
SAWMILLERS

"PROTIM"
PROCESSORS

OWENS, PECK & CO. LIMITED

48 RIMROSE ROAD,
BOOTLE, 20,
LANCS.
'Phone BOOTLE 4101 (5 lines)

Owens Peck & Co. Ltd were timber importers, merchants and sawmillers. They had a number of timber yards in Bootle and Liverpool. This advertising postcard is for No. 48 Rimrose Road.

Massive pieces of timber brought by sea from all corners of the world are seen in the background. Two members of the Owens Peck family, along with the timber yard foreman, walk through the yard.

St Mary's, Bootle's first parish church, stood on Derby Road at the junction of Church Street. It was built in 1827 and had twin towers which were used as navigational aids for sailing ships coming into the River Mersey. These were later replaced by a single spire. This beautiful church was destroyed during the May blitz when a German bomber, caught in the cables of a barrage balloon, caught fire the latter fell onto the roof of the church setting it alight and burning it to the ground. Later, all the grave stones were laid flat and a garden of rest created.

1918 saw a Peace Day victory march and service at St Mary's church, Derby Road. All denominations attended including many Service personnel. During the widening of Rimrose and Derby Roads in 1973 the remains of 1,138 persons were reinterred in Bootle Cemetery.

Kirk Street ran from Church View to Derby Road. This was a mainly catholic area, with a small number of Protestants residing there. There were a lot of large families living here including John and Sarah Brady who lived at No. 43. There were nine members of the Brady family. During the celebration to mark the Jubilee of St Winifred's church all the streets were highly decorated. All walls, windows, doors, gutters, downspouts and any other space available were decorated with religious artefacts. Everyone in the street posed for this photograph.

Seaforth Street was also decorated for the visit of Archbishop Downey to St Winifred's. As money was hard to come by the paper decorations were coloured with anything that had a colour in it, for example 'Reckets Blue' dye and Cochineal beetle blood. The children wearing their Communion clothes would walk in procession around the area, carrying lighted candles and singing religious music, in the hope of collecting money for the church.

In 1846 a dispensary was built, but was replaced by a house in Berry Street in 1866. A purpose-built hospital was built on Derby Road in close proximity of the docks, at a cost of over £4,200. Although damaged during the Second World War it stayed open to administer to the sick and injured. It sadly closed down in 1976 and remained empty for a while until it was purchased by a testing laboratory, and renamed Masthouse.

For the benefit of patients and staff, live shows were staged at the hospital. In 1952 the 'Orrell Mandoliers' performed there. Their leader, Ted Martin (in the striped jacket), and the other members go through their routine.

This elevated view was taken from the roof of Bootle Hospital, just after the war. William Henry Street almost stands alone amongst the cleared debris of bombed houses. The Knowsley public house was known locally as the 'Blue House'. It was closed and demolished in the early 1970s to allow for the widening of Derby Road. Another pub to bite the dust was the Old Toll Bar at the junction of Derby Road and Millers Bridge.

The bakery of John Looney at 290 Derby Road, at the junction of Dundas Street. Mrs Looney takes a welcome break and stands at the doorway. Like many of the streets in that area between Derby Road and Regent Road, Dundas Street was built to accommodate the influx of workers that mainly came from Ireland and Wales to work on the docks. It was one of the poorest streets in the area along with Howe Street, Beresford Street, Raleigh Street and Effingham Street. Large families were crammed into these hovels. They were also a magnet for prostitutes, thieves, pick-pockets and the like who preyed on these migrant workers and their families.

Dundas Street, along with the streets mentioned above, was demolished and the land purchased by Harland & Wolff on which to build their works. Now this is just a short cul-de-sac with only one business. The Island Bed Company has the corner building that was once part of Harland & Wolff's canteen.

At the other end of the block is another cul-de-sac by the name of Beresford Street. This
street was once teeming with all sorts of criminals. Prostitutes plied their trade in the alleys
and inside these filthy hovels. Originally named Lyons Street this street was the scene of
a horrific murder. In one of these slums two prostitutes were brutally murdered, by three
seamen. It was dubbed the 'Teapot Murders' after the tea company. The street name was later
changed to Beresford Street.

Derby Road, at the borough boundary with Liverpool. To the right is Dacre Street and
opposite is Bedford Place, with Martins Bank on the corner. This picture was taken in the
early 1950s and there are still some derelict sites. In the distance can just be seen Esk Street
and Derby Road Bridewell.

Crossing the canal at Bedford Place brings you into Brasenose Road. This photograph is the only one known to exist of the premises belonging to Seanor & Co. Ltd, firelighter manufacturers. George Seanor, the owner, stands watching one of his horse and carts being loaded with firelighters. The company was eventually sold to Bryant & May matchmakers.

Communion at St Alexander's. One of the churches in St John's Road was St Alexander's, which was opened on 8 December 1867 by the Right Reverend Alexander Goss, second Bishop of Liverpool. This church was loved by many, especially by Teresa Higginson (see p. 39). The church was destroyed by bombs of the German Luftwaffe during the May blitz.

Above: This rare photograph of the interior of the original church, which cost £3,750 to build. Its first parish priest was Father Edward Powell. The last priest to officiate there before the bombing was Canon Kelly.

Right: Teresa Higginson was a teacher at St Alexander's school and she developed stigmata on her hands and feet, and on her head the marks of the crown of thorns. From 1879 she had many visions of Our Lord. She stated that 'Our Lords wish is that she makes it known to the world, to the devotion of His Sacred Heart, at a seat of divine worship'. She died on 15 February 1905, in her sixtieth year. She was buried at St Winifred's churchyard Neston-cum-Parkgate, Cheshire.

TERESA HIGGINSON'S LAST WORDS.

"Do not fear, dear child, but put your hand with loving confidence into your Father's hand and He will guide you safely through every path, and where the road is rough and stony He will carry you in His arms.

Buried in St. Winifride's Church Yard, Neston-cum-Parkgate, Chesh.

The last St Alexander's church was built in 1957 and opened by Canon Charles Taylor, parish priest of St Richard's, in Mirander Road, Bootle. This was in his Jubilee year. Crowds lined the route to the church as the motorcade went around the parish and on to St Alexander's for the opening ceremony and Mass. Due to falling attendances and cost of upkeep it was forced to close and was demolished in 1991.

There was an active social life at St Alexander's and they had many sports teams including the netball team. In 1926 they won the knockout championship and the league Championship. The girls and trophies are pictured in the church grounds.

The annual works photograph was taken at the premises of James Cooke, saw and file makers, just inside the main entrance. Top left in the bowler hat is the owner himself, Mr James Cooke. The works backed onto the railway line near to Oriel Road station.

St John's (Church of England) stood on St John's Road. It was a very impressive church internally but rather austere on the outside. Bootle Corporation laid out the churchyard as a public garden.

Left: The Revd Breeze was the vicar of St John's in the 1930s. The church was another to fall foul of the Luftwaffe during the Second World War. The scene was recorded by Jeromes of London Road, Liverpool, well-known photographers.

Below: The women's group in St John's church was very active in fund raising, and enjoyed days out. This outing was to the Calderstones Park, Liverpool in the 1920s.

St James' and St Winifred's churches joined in procession on 12 June 1910 and walked the parish. They are walking down Millers Bridge, approaching Derby Road. This photograph was taken outside the Royal Standard public house.

This postcard announces the sad news of the death of Edith McIntyre on 1 October 1941. The obverse side shows Bootle Town Hall which opened in 1882 at a cost of £37,352. Far right is the main post office, next to Bootle magistrates courts. Next is the entrance to Bootle police headquarters.

Above: This was the public and police entrance to Bootle police station. Also the entrance for the reception of prisoners. The yard led to various offices, including the CID office and garages.

Right: Two Bootle County Borough police raw recruits, pictured during their initial thirteen weeks training at Bruche, Warrington in 1965. They are Graham McDonald (left) and Peter Woolley. After initial training they returned to their force as Probationary Constables.

Above: A group of Bootle 'bobbies' in 1911, with civilian typist Miss May Leslie. They are PC 5 J. Grinrod, PC 19 Lawson, PC 56 Sayle, PC 17 Ashton, PC 9 Jackson, PC 32 Burton, PC 51 Gibbs, PC 6 Harper, PC 16 Starkey, PC 30 Waugh. Front: PC 37 Raven, PC 52 Marsden.

Left: Inspector Edwin 'Ted' Carter looking very smart in his uniform, complete with signalling stick. He lived with his family at 31 Litherland Road, Bootle, on the corner of Park Street. It was once the home of William Pickles Hartley of jam-making fame.

Detective Inspector Ted Carter at his desk in the CID office at Oriel Road, Bridewell. When Bootle Stadium opened Ted Carter was made clerk of the course. He retired in 1938 and was appointed Chief of Work Police & Security at Air Ministry, Rootes aircraft factory in Speke.

Bootle Police swimming team. Inset left: David Gilliland, Harry Jeffrey. Inset right: Jock Aitkin, Wynn Williams. Left to right, back row: -?-, Harry Smith, ? Williams, Bob Hayes, G. Buck, Ted Jones. Middle row: Arthur Dyke, Jimmy ?, Sid Jones, Jess Bailey, Bill Cottier, Les Cairns, Norman Boulton, Jack Johnson, Bill Gilbertson. Front row: Gordon Clark, Frank Rooney, -?-, W.A. Gale (builder), Tom Bell (Chief Constable), J. Dobson, Tom Smith, Fred Evans.

In 1936 there was a Government Inspection of the Bootle Police Force. Chief Constable Tom Bell (in full uniform) and Mayor of Bootle, Alderman J.S. Kelly, along with the Police Committee are seen inspecting the new cycle patrol, ten in all, in the rear yard at Oriel Road. Behind them is the Black Maria. It was built by Garlick Burrell & Edwards Works in Hawthorne Road.

The Merseyside Civil Defence medal presentation. Medals were handed out fro bravery during the May blitz in Bootle. From left to right: Robert Pritchard, Rescue Squad (George Medal), PC T.J. McCarthy, Bootle Police (George Medal), Cheif Constable Tom Bell, Sgt D.C. Forshaw, Bootle Police (George Medal) and The Mayor of Bootle, Alderman J.S. Kelly congratulating the medalists. PC Victor J. Scott, Bootle Police (George Medal) could not attend as he was in hospital.

Above: Bootle police formed the guard of honour in 1954 for the opening of St Monica's Catholic church, Fernhill Road. They included: Jess Bailey, Ronnie Henshaw, Sid Jones, Ronnie Ross, Fred Tomlinson, Bill Gwynell, John Knapp, Jim Scholfield.

Left; Merseyside police helmet plate. Police long service and good conduct medal were presented to Constable Peter Woolley after twenty-two years' service.

Previous Page: The Merseyside Civil Defence medal presentation, for bravery during the May blitz in Bootle. Left to right: Robert Pritchard, rescue squad, Turner Avenue, Bootle (George Medal), PC T.J. McCarthy, Bootle police (George Medal), Chief Constable Tom Bell, Sergeant D.C. Forshaw, Bootle police (George Medal), Mayor of Bootle Alderman J.S. Kelly. PC Victor J. Scott, Bootle police (George Medal) could not attend as he was in hospital.

In Oriel Road was the entrance to Balliol Road railway station. This building was the booking office. When the station closed in 1954 it was empty for a while then it became the NALGO social club. Over the years it was broken into and was vandalized. In 1999 it was set on fire.

On the top floor of Bootle Town Hall was the Borough switch board. Manning it in this snapshot are Marie Miley (left) and Jean Bell (daughter of Tom Bell, Chief Constable).

Left: The Royal Marines band marches up and down Oriel Road in front of the town hall in preparation for the arrival of Queen Elizabeth and Prince Philip, during the Battle of the Atlantic commemorations.

Below: Bootle NALGO ladies hockey team in 1959 in Bootle Town Hall with the Mayor J.C. Heavey. The team won the Diamine Cup and runners-up championship (Sturla's Cup). From left to right, front row: Miss Lalla McDermot, Francis Yates, the Mayor, G. Watts, M. Johnson, M. Loftus, J. Murphy, H. Preston. Back Row: R. J. Dinwoodie, J. McMahon, S. Sheridan, D. Caton. V. Abbott, J. Stafford.

Bootle Historical Society were invited to Bootle Town Hall for a tour of this beautiful and historic building. They were met by the Mayor and Mayoress of Sefton, Councillor Terry and Mrs Valerie Francis, who gave the guided tour. During the tour the group were privileged to have tea with the Mayor and Mayoress in the Mayors parlour, and were photographed with them on the impressive staircase.

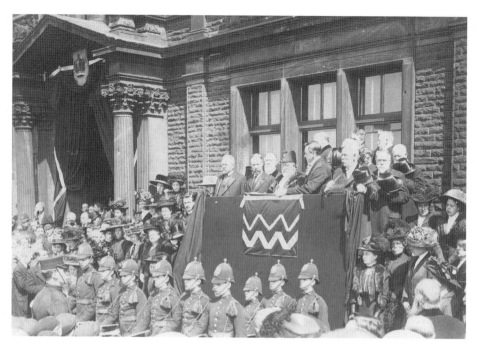

On 10 May 1910 a crowd gathered in Oriel Road outside the town hall to hear the Mayor of Bootle, Hugh Carruthers Esq., read out the Proclamation of King George V in the presence of other civic dignitaries.

In Oriel Road a covered dias was erected in readiness for the arrival of King George V and Queen Mary on their courtesy visit to Bootle in 1913 after opening the first phase of Gladstone Dock. Prominent persons were presented to the Royal couple, including Mr and Mrs Peter Ashcroft.

Two chairs were specially made for the occasion of the Royal visit to Bootle is 1913. They had a brass plate attached to the front of each. This one reads: 'Queens Chair. Presented to the Mayor and Mayoress of Bootle W.H. Clemmy Esq and Mrs Clemmy on the occasion of the visit of their Majesties King George V and Queen Mary to Bootle 11 July 1913.'

During their stay in Liverpool and Bootle in March 1914 King George V and Queen Mary were the guests of Lord Derby at Knowsley Hall. The Royal party pose for a photograph with Lord and Lady Derby and other prominent guests in the grounds of Knowsley Hall.

When the second and final phase of Gladstone Dock was opened in 1927 King George V and Queen Mary again came to Bootle to open it. They arrived at Oriel Road railway station where they were met by a guard of honour of soldiers and police, as seen here outside the *Bootle Times* office and print works. A VIP grandstand had been erected next to it.

The Royal party having arrived at Oriel Road railway station were presented by the Mayor Alderman Clemmy to Bootle's May Queen of the time, Miss Pauline West-Sadler, and her retinue. Draped in banners and flags is the *Bootle Times* shop, office and works.

Bootle's Oriel Road railway station as seen in 1951 from Millers Bridge. Three platforms are in use, with the left-hand one set aside for goods traffic. The nearest line went to Bankfield Goods yard (which closed in 1965). Houses and buildings on the left are in Berry Street.

The same view seen from pretty much the same position but in 2004. The platform canopies have gone along with part of the main platforms. The lines on the left are disused and one has been taken up. The houses and buildings in Berry Street have been replaced by industrial sites.

A close–up view of Oriel Road railway station in 1971. Now just a shadow of its former self, it looks in a sorry state. All of the canopies have long gone, along with toilets, waiting rooms, kiosk, and so on.

Awful Calamity.

A Liver (Rara. avis) was found on the border of Bootle swollen to an enormous size having swallowed a tramway route. Although large doses of community of interest were administered, the bird died on Tuesday the 7th of July 1903. Funeral procession to night at 6.30, headed by the Mayor & corporation of Bootl

Written on a chalk board in 1903, this supposedly funny message by an unknown writer was photographed by William Thomas Wright (W & Co.).

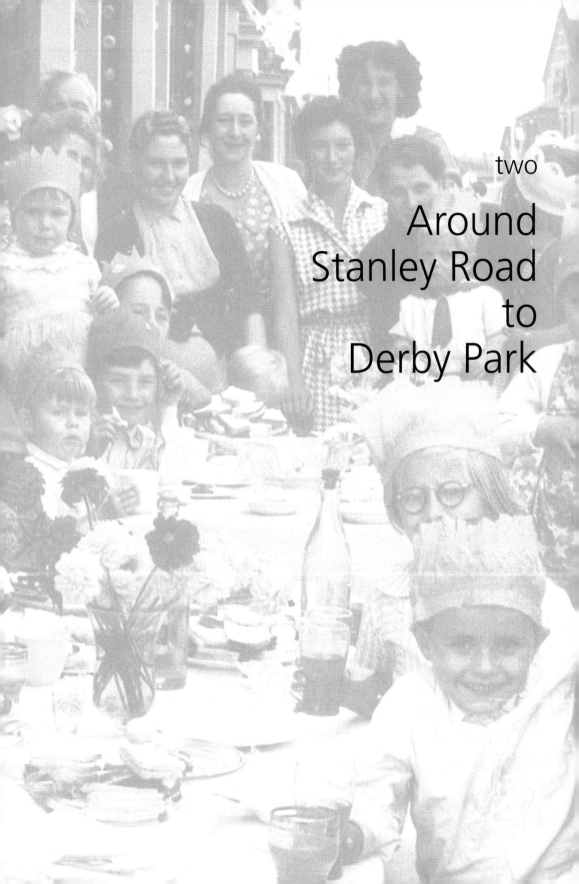

two

Around Stanley Road to Derby Park

Bootle Baths, Balliol Road were built in 1888 at a cost of £14,849. In their day they were the finest baths in the north of England. In winter months the large swimming bath was covered over and used as a gymnasium. The gentlemans salt water bath was 100ft long and 80ft wide. There were Roman, hot air, vapour and other private baths. The baths closed in 1998 and fell derelict. Efforts to sell the property failed and it has since been demolished, except for the façade, which remains.

Bootle Secondary School for Girls, Balliol Road, built on the site of Balliol Road gardens. It was opened 13 September 1910 by Sir Benjamin Johnson. The Mayor of the time was Hugh Carruthers.

Bootle Technical School viewed from Pembroke Road in 1912. The school was built at a cost of £25,770 and opened by Lord Derby in 1900. Upon opening, the number of registered pupils was 1,500. It also incorporated the girls secondary school next door.

In 1913 the school yard in Pembroke Road was used for the rehearsal of the 7th Kings regiment based at Park Street Barracks. They were practising for the visit of King George V and Queen Mary. These soldiers and bandsmen were in full dress uniform. All of these men served in the First World War from 1914 and many made the supreme sacrifice, sadly only a few returned at the end of hostilities.

Right: In Balliol Road and Merton Road some very fine houses were built, including this one in Balliol Road. The family that lived there in 1905 were Mr and Mrs Eales.

Below: Kings Gardens, Stanley Road was built on the site of stables that were used by Liverpool Corporation Public Transport for the horses that pulled the trams. Behind the war memorial is Emmanuel Congregational Church, which opened in 1876 and could accommodate 750 persons.

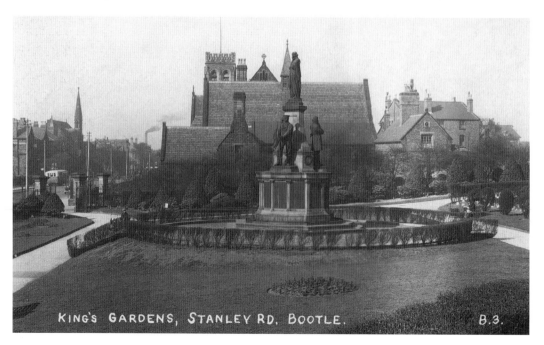

KING'S GARDENS, STANLEY RD. BOOTLE.   B.3.

Left: Bootle's War Memorial, Stanley Gardens, was unveiled by Major James Burnie MC on 15 October 1922. The name of every Bootle person who has died in conflict for their country has been included on this war memorial.

Below: A longer view of Kings Gardens, with the statue to Edward VII. From left to right can be seen John Gerratty sculptor of gravestones, Bootle School of Art on the corner of Balliol Road and Stanley Road, then the spire of Calvanistic Methodist church on Trinity Road. The church has now closed and been turned into offices with the address Pinnacle House. To the left of the church is Bootle school for the blind.

In Stanley Road, opposite Bedford Road was the newsagents of the Fearnley brothers. This postcard of 1920 shows the van in which they delivered their newspapers taking part in the Bootle May Day Procession.

Looking into the borough at the boundary with Kirkdale is this view of Stanley Road in the 1950s. Note the prefabs constructed to house those left homeless after the bombing of the Second World War. The prefabs were meant to be temporary but some were still being used in the 1970s. On the left is now Mowbray Court, 'Anchor' sheltered accommodation.

Above: In Bootle, apart from the main places of worship, there were also small chapels and Mission Halls. On the corner of Mirander Road and Rosalind Street was this Wesleyan chapel. This is believed to be the only photograph in existence of the interior. The chapel was destroyed by an incendiary bomb in the Second World War.

Right: In Mirander Road, as with other areas, the corner shop was the cornerstone of the community. Miss Roache and her mongrel dog are pictured outside her shop.

Another view of this corner shop in Mirander Road. Miss Roache, a neighbour and a group of children pose outside her shop.

It's party time in Mirander Road. The occasion was the Jubilee celebration for the local priest of St Richards church (seen in background), Canon Kelly. The tables were set up outside the Victoria public house.

Boyle family members Kathleen, Violet (mother) and Alan pose outside their home at No. 49 Beatrice Street. They were celebrating Canon Kelly's Jubilee.

As previously mentioned, after the war the shortage of living accommodation was 'temporarily' alleviated by pre-fabricated houses. Some were erected on bombed sites, whilst the local parks also provided a venue. This one was in South Park, near to Wadham Road. Some prefabs lasted into the 1980s.

Hawthorne Road, seen from Sydney Road, looking towards Wadham Road and further on Bedford Road, and then the Bootle boundary. Other roads on the left include Clare Road, Downing Road and Gonville Road. The shop behind the postbox is Mrs Jane Thomas' drapers.

Trinity Road looking up towards Hawthorne Road and Trinity church. The church opened its doors in 1887 and could accommodate 820 people. It closed in 1980 and was subsequently demolished. Sheltered accommodation was built on the site.

One of the main thoroughfares dissecting the borough, Merton Road, is one of the oldest roads in Bootle. It is the location for Bootle's oldest house, Lord Derby's shooting lodge, which was built in the eighteenth century. At the top is Bootle parish church, Christ Church built in 1886. In front of it is a drinking fountain which has been located on Southport Road, near to Breeze Hill.

Beautiful ornamental gates at the Oxford Road entrance of Derby Park. They were designed by Brierleys of Staffordshire and cost £600. This postcard of the gates and the park shows the decorations that were put up to celebrate the Coronation of King Edward VII on 9 August 1902.

On entering Derby Park through the Oxford Road gates the path leads past the memorial statue to William Poulsom. In 1880 he proposed setting up a Bootle police force (it was actually established in 1887) In his time he was the largest employer in Bootle. He died 30 January 1903 and his statue is the only public memorial to a private citizen in Bootle. Poulsom Drive is named after him.

Derby Park grew its own flowers and plants which were cultivated in their two very large greenhouses in the park. Sadly both of them have now gone. The path then leads down to the steps and balustrade.

Viewed from the lower pathway these marble steps and the balustrade made an excellent divide between the two halves of the park. At one time there were two cannons at the top of the steps which were given to the park by Colonel Sandys, the local MP. It is not known which war they were from or what happened to them when they were taken from the park.

DERBY PARK BOOTLE P S 2448

On reaching the bottom of the steps the path leads to the popular bandstand, where of an evening and Sunday afternoon the populace would be entertained by orchestras, bands and choirs.

Above: This bridge pictured in 1912 was the main structure that crossed over Derby Park lake from the bandstand to Earl Road entrance. The bridge is still there. Although the lake has long gone, there are plans to bring it back to the park.

Left: Sent through the post in 1929 this sepia postcard shows the rustic ornamental rock arch. For many a kid this is where they fought the Indians, or it was a castle, or maybe a pirate ship in their games.

Outside the park entrance at Oxford Road, at its junction with Worcester Road, stands a single-decker bus on the 57 route with its driver, conductor, and passengers posing for the camera.

Christ Church School in 1912, with children all smartly dressed and attentive. No doubt many readers will recall those green-tiled walls with an abundance of pictures upon them, the desks with the cast-iron frames which bruised many a knee and the ink wells in which black powder and water were mixed to make the ink.

Christ Church School for Boys in 1916 Standard VI. Notice the old-style Eton collars, and the mixture of ties and bow ties.

Merton Road in 1923, looking rather dark in this sadly poor quality postcard. To the left of Christ Church is Oxford Road, whilst coming back this way are the gate posts on the left of Lord Derby's shooting lodge, and a bit further this way is Litherland Road.

A rare photograph of Litherland Road at its junction with Merton Road, looking towards Park Street and Bootle Village. At the junction a lady and gentleman stop and look towards the camera, whilst an errand boy goes on his way. Buildings from the right include Bootle circulating library, the Jawbone public house and Irwins.

The same view except it shows a cold, icy, snow-laden day. Most people have stayed indoors, but deliveries still have to be made. In the distance is Park Street and Bootle Village.

Miss Pauline Carter (daughter of Ted Carter, police inspector), plays happily in the front garden of her home on the corner of Park Street and Litherland Road. Along Park Street, just visible, is the preserves factory.

On the other corner of Park Street was Shepherds chemists, seen here gaily decorated for the coronation of King Edward VI in 1902. Mrs Shepherd is seen gazing into the side window of the shop.

This modern view in 2004 shows the house that Pauline Carter lived in. As mentioned previously (p. 45) William Pickles Hartley, of Hartley's jam, once lived here. He had a jam factory in Pine Grove between 1874 and 1886. Across the road can be seen the modern houses that replaced Shepherds chemists shop.

Off Park Street is Spring Grove, all decked out for a street party in 1937 to celebrate the coronation of King George V. The chimney visible is of the preserves factory, which was also the egg factory.

Tom Aizlewood (1873-1942) and his wife Polly (1876-1946) sit in their back yard at 45 Litherland Road. Tom established the firm of T.A. Aizlewood, which traded from their home.

Walter Aizlewood, son of Tom and Polly, in the back yard of his home in 1911, checking the next days, orders for his handcart hire. When his parents died he became the sole owner of the firm. The handcarts were kept in the back yard.

Opposite Aizlewood's was a blacksmiths forge. This copy of a painting seems to be the only record of this business.

This painting was done in enamel, by someone who lived in Bootle Village. On the left near the canal is Langtons yard. Homes on the left included, No. 127 Mrs Horton (Bargee), No. 129 was Pinningtons, No. 131 Mr (donkey) Jones, No. 133 Johannsons. The latter house had a stable at the rear, accommodating a horse named 'Alice'. There were also chickens, ducks and a pig. On the right of Litherland Road was King Dicks, O'Keefes (fruit and vegetables) with a sweet shop next door.

King Dicks public house on Litherland Road, Bootle village was an integral part of the social life of the village. Pctured in the parlour one Saturday evening is Carl Johannson talking to Rose Scott (identified by 'X' above their heads).

Above: Young Stephen Ford in his back garden, which backed onto the canal. A bargee manoeuvres his barge around a bend in the canal. The building on the other side of the canal was the haulage firm of A. Wright of Elm Street.

Below: The chimney of William's toffee factory stands tall on the day that it was to be demolished in 1999. This was the final part as the rest had already been demolished. On the day it was built local children were allowed to climb the iron ladder inside the chimney to the top and wave at their mums and dads below.

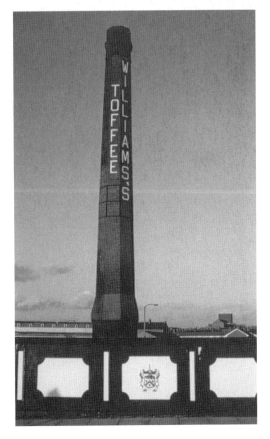

Carl Johannson stands outside No. 24 Elm Street with daughter Alice aged seven years, and Lily Cooke aged five years. Carl was a master steeplejack until an accident prevented him from working, hence the support belt.

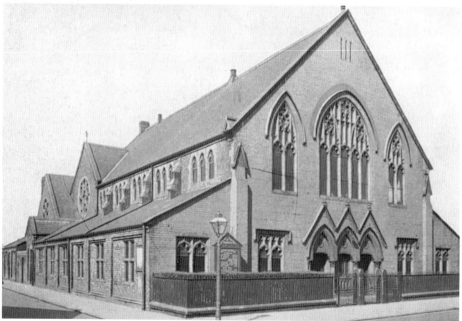

Ash Street Baptist church stands on the corner of Litherland Road. Built in 1886 within Bootle-cum-Linacre, this lovely church, like so many on Merseyside, has difficulty keeping going, with congregation diminishing and costs for its upkeep rising.

A view in 1926 of the interior of the church, with the beautiful inscription painted above the organ. Sadly most of this has gone. Also the forms have been replaced by pews.

Arthur Wright ran a haulage contractors business in Elm Street. He also ran Wrights Coaches. Alongside one of them are, left to right: Reginald Fyfe Simpson (driver), Arthur Wright and Harold Hinks. The remainder are Wright family members.

In 1960 this is what the top of Marsh Lane looked like. The chimney of 'Hunters' Handy Hams was a local landmark. From Litherland Road: on the right was a house and stable owned by Mr and Mrs John Large, next came 'Stanley Buildings' which incorporated the Stanley Social Club gymnasium, Liverpool *Daily Post* and *Echo* office, Joseph Corrish, boot repairer, and Mrs Erikson's sweets and tobacconists shop. On the left was Parr's builders merchants. Although Parr's have since moved, the building remains.

From Marsh Lane into Stanley Road, the main shopping area in 1960. Behind the Ford Anglia car were the gentleman's public conveniences, F. Taylor and Sons (Liverpool) Ltd commercial motor agents, Thompson's funeral directors, Robert Rogerson butcher.

Left: The well-loved Metropole Theatre opened in March 1911. It saw many stars of the day such as Charlie Chaplin, Gracie Fields, Issy Bonn and Arthur Tracy. It was sadly destroyed during the May blitz.

Below: Photocall on stage at the Metropole Theatre for the Bootle Operatic Society's production. Phylis Willetts is third from the left. She now lives in Windsor Court, Orrell.

Bootle Operatic Society production of *The Pirates of Penzance* by Gilbert and Sullivan. This time they take a photocall during their dress rehearsal. Many local amateur companies performed there. The most popular shows were the circus and the pantomimes at Christmas time.

Strand Road ran from Regent Road through to Stanley Road. Between Washington Street and Stanley Road was the main shopping area. This postcard looking down Strand Road shows the Langton Hotel on the corner with Stanley Road. The No. 23 tram trundles its way towards Seaforth.

Strand Road, Bootle

May 5th 1906

Strand Road was reputed to be one of the best shopping roads in Lancashire. This was mainly due to the influx of seamen from the nearby docks, looking for cheap items of clothing to take home to their countries to resell. All the streets off Strand Road were named after American towns and cities.

A busy Strand Road in 1962 on a Saturday afternoon, with housewives rushing to get their shopping done. A BSA motorcycle rides past (notice no helmet), a Lambretta scooter with full windscreen, a Morris van, plus two Corporation buses.

A less busy day in Strand Road. A Ford Zepher saloon, 629 FKD, is parked with a Hillman, 730 DLV. Tom Barber was born above Melia's shop on the corner of Virginia Street in 1946. Next door was the fried fish dealer of Mrs Helen McComish.

A very early view of Stanley Road, posted in 1906. It's so quiet people can stand in the road without fear of being knocked down. Irwins stores is on the corner of Little Strand Road, next door was Taylors Tobacconists, Harry Charnocks bakery and Soloman Goldstein glass merchant.

Same view, only fifty-six years later. Swifts furnishers have replaced Irwins, next is Coombes and Co. shoe repairers, Josie Goffman drapers, County Furnishers and Comptons opticians. A Foden lorry waits at the traffic lights.

Looking up Stanley Road from Strand Road, on the right was Irwins (Tesco) grocers. Next door was Montague Burtons outfitters, above this shop was a dance hall. It had one of the first sprung dance floors in Liverpool. One of the bands that played there was Frank Woods and his Roseland dance band. Instruments played were banjo, saxophone, trumpet, drums, piano and trombone. Next door was the store of F. W. Woolworth.

On the other side of Stanley Road the first shop is Martins the cleaners, then Beatties hairdressers, S. Reece and Son Ltd confectioners, Anne Bell (Liverpool) Ltd gowns, Ray's china and glass, W.T. Jones and Son Ltd bird food dealers, Brighter Home Stores Ltd wallpaper merchants.

At the top of Sullivans Brow, Stanley Road crosses the Leeds Liverpool Canal. From this bridge we are looking towards Coffee House Bridge. On the right of the canal side are George Bowring and Son pork butchers, and Applebys flour mills. Left of the canal is land which was part of Criddles syrup and treacle manufacturers. It then became Merton Grove treacle factory. The Buckingham Social Club and car park now occupies this site.

What do
you know about

CRIDDLE'S
OLD FASHIONED
BLACK
TREACLE

and its uses?

CRIDDLES
FINEST
GOLDEN SYRUP

MANUFACTURED BY
W.E. CRIDDLE & SON L? C ROSE

and its uses?

Perhaps very little
SEND FOR OUR FREE BOOKLET OF RECIPES AND
HEALTH HINTS TO:-

W. E. CRIDDLE & SON, Ltd.
Liverpool, 1

KINDLY PASS ON THIS RECORD
TO A FRIEND
S.D.29.

Right: There were various ways to advertise a business. Criddles came up with the novel idea of promoting their products on a record disc. It appears to be made of cardboard with a wax-type covering – how it was played is not known!

Below: Washington Parade crosses the canal near Merton Grove. The two Merseyside police motorcyclists are Paul Kavanagh (right) and an unknown officer. They were part of the escort for the band of the Royal Marines on route to Bootle Town Hall. The blocks of flats are off Marsh Lane and include Stanley House, Mersey House and Chestnut House.

Washington Parade with the Royal Marines band during the 50th Anniversary celebrations of the end of the Battle of the Atlantic. On the left are Stella Maris, the Seamans Mission, Stanley Social Club, and Georges Tavern. Very prominent in the background is Johnsons Brothers dyers and cleaners (soon to close).

At the other end of Washington Parade was Bullens Terrace, seen here from Bootle New Strand Station. The railway line runs under the road. This line ran from the docks under Stanley Road, Marsh Lane, Southport Road and through to Fazakerley North Junction. This line was closed and filled in on 3rd June 1972. The building on the left is Marsh Lane police station.

The Palace cinema, Marsh Lane was the first purpose-built cinema in Bootle. It opened on 19 October 1912 and originally could accommodate nearly 1,000 patrons. This was reduced to 722 when forms in the front rows were replaced by tip-up seats. The first film shown was *The Lady Diver* plus full supporting programme with musical accompaniment. The first 'talkie' film shown was *In Old Arizona* on 29 June 1929.

The interior of the Palace. It had a raked auditorium, so that patrons had an unimpeded view of the screen. Ventilation was a new innovation with the air being circulated every ten minutes through a system of fans, ventilation and grills. Radiators kept patrons warm during colder nights. The cinema closed on 26 April 1958.

The building fell into disuse for nearly two years, until May Logan 'Auntie Margaret' persuaded Bootle council to let the ex-Palace cinema for use as The Bootle Social Centre for the children of Bootle. It reopened in December 1959. Two of her staunch supporters, who also helped run the centre, were Mr and Mrs Wanless.

Due to rising costs and lack of support it was reluctantly decided that the social centre would have to close. It was very sad as many dedicated people had spent many years giving up their spare time for the children of Bootle. It eventually closed in the 1970s. Again it fell into disuse and suffered from vandals. Plans were made to sell the building and demolish it. The demolition took place in 1999 and these last two photographs show the building on the day before it was demolished.

On the site of the Palace cinema and Bootle Social Centre the 'New Medical Centre' was built. To its right is Marsh Lane police station, which opened in 1974 to replace the ageing Oriel Road police station, which had been open since 1887.

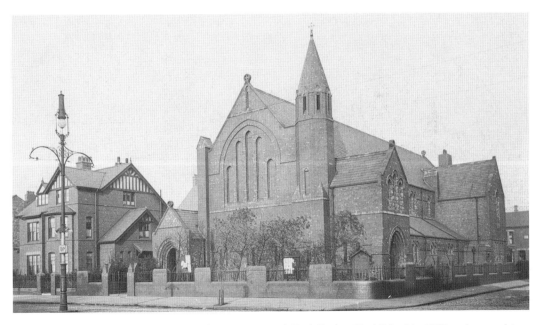

St Mathew's church, Stanley Road, opposite North Park Lodge. Established in 1887 and opened in 1891 it could accommodate 600 people. This beautiful church was always well attended through the years, but like so many churches upkeep costs have risen and it is difficult to maintain the building in its former state. Part of it is used by community groups, with learning centres and a support group.

Before television and other modern distractions, churches provided a very varied social life for local people, including beetle drives, whist drives, socials and sports events. St Mathew's had its own hockey team with both male and female members, here seen with church officials in the 1911/12 season.

May Logan, who was 'Auntie Margaret' to countless numbers of Bootle children, was a staunch and tireless worker for the good of Bootle. Her parents were well known in the borough as they owned a fish and chip shop. She worked on the *Bootle Times* newspaper for many years, working her way up to Editor, a Justice of the Peace, and sat on various committees for charities. She was honoured by the Queen with an MBE for her services to Bootle. She died on 15 December 1995 and was laid to rest in Bootle cemetery.

three

Bootle May Day
Demonstrations

Miss Alice Parry aged twelve years, was the first Bootle May Queen in 1896. The Bootle May Day Demonstration took place over three days: Friday, Saturday and Monday. It was not held on a Sunday. Alice Parry was the daughter of Mr W.H. Parry, Chairman of the May Day Committee.

The most staunch supporter of the Bootle May Day Demonstration was May Logan. She was the hardest worker, not only behind the scenes, but on the three days it took place she was there still at the front organising and making sure everything ran smoothly. The jewelled pin shown here was presented to each May Queen upon being crowned. It was her personal present to Bootle's Queen.

Miss Kathleen Miller was May Queen in 1907. She is shown in the main arena with Ruth Sanders, Dowager Queen alongside her, followed by her retinue and guided by a member of the organising committee.

These lovely girls were photographed in the studio of William Thomas Wright (W & Co.) at No. 324 Stanley Road, Bootle.

The ever popular Bootle Morris Dancers go through their routine prior to entering the parade. They were trained by Mr David White.

This beautifully turned out shire horse, with Hawthorne Road School who were depicting 'Wild Roses', gained third prize in class 7 in 1907. The scene was photographed behind Bootle Baths.

Right: Miss Mary Agnes Dunne
was May Queen in 1908. She
was the daughter of Robert H.
Dunne, confectioner of No. 181
Marsh Lane. Her photograph
was taken by Harry Dowden,
'Parkside' studio, Stanley Road.

Below; On arrival at North
Park in her carriage, Mary
Agnes Dunne and her Dowager
Queen, Kathleen Miller,
paraded around the main arena
with her retinue, on the way to
Mary being crowned.

Above: Looking resplendent in their uniforms, the Bootle cycle club pose at the rear of a house in Merton Road prior to joining the 1908 May procession. In the centre of the second row is a girl named Maggie.

Left: William Thomas Wright (W & Co.) took most of the May Queen photographs over the years. This is Violet Wilson, pictured in 1911, in his studio in Stanley Road.

Crowds line Stanley Road on Sullivans Brow during the 1912 May procession. Near Carolina Street the Girl Guides march through the crowds. The May Queen was Christina McDonald.

The 1913 May Queen, Miss Ella Phipps, with Dowager Queen, Christina McDonald, and main attendants. The crown bearer (right) has a cushion with the May Queen's initials (E.P.) embroidered on it.

Above: All manner of vehicles took part in the parades. This fire engine, E.M. 919, named 'Eachus', was driven by leading fireman Mark Eady in 1920. Money was collected in nets attached to long poles so the firemen would not have to get down for money and then climb back each time.

Left: Miss Lettie Wharton, daughter of George E. Wharton, confectioner, was May Queen in 1920. She is pictured in the garden of her home.

'Sweet Peas' was the float theme for Orrell Primary school in 1921. Their school yard was the scene for this photograph. In the group is Miss Annie Woods of No. 59 Glynne Street, Orrell.

Bootle Corporation Electric Department produced this 'charabanc' powered by the feet of twenty people. Registered number U.G.O. 2, it advertised holidays in 'Bright, Breezy and Better Bootle'. Following behind in Bibby's Lane was a foot-powered by-plane.

A Zulu and Minstrel Band was conjured up by a group of council workers in their Pine Grove Depot. Behind them is a refuse destructor and chimney.

A group of children from Linacre School are dressed in costume ready for maypole dancing. Annie Woods, aged twelve years, is somewhere in the picture.

May Day, Bootle, 1923. A group of floats travel up Merton Road from Oriel Road. Leading them are 'Thistles', though from which school they came is not known. Attentive mothers walk alongside each float looking after their children.

May Day, Bootle, 1924. Contestants in the fancy dress competition include: doll in a box, cowboys and indians, Charlie Chaplins, gypsies, clowns, and puck matchbox among others. The tall girl in centre is Annastacia 'Stacie' Cowperthwaite.

Maypole dancers in 1924. These dancers were from Linacre School and they make a pretty picture.
Annie Woods is pictured on the third row from front, first girl from the left.

Maypole dancers, six years later, in 1930. Sophie Hammond aged ten years, of No. 8 Staly Street
is pictured at the far left of the front row. Elsie Blundell is on the back row, far right, and Daisey
Crockett from Elizabeth Road, Orrell is also pictured.

BOOTLE MAY DAY 1927. ANKLE COMPETITION. T.R. No 28.

Above: The 1927 Mayor of Bootle, Councillor Frederick King, examines an ankle with a number of amused ladies in a mock prettiest ankle competition.

Right: Miss Pauline West Sadler poses by a trellis arch in the garden of her parents home in 1927. She was the daughter of butcher, John West Sadler whose shop was in Strand Road.

MISS PAULINE
WEST SADLER.
BOOTLE MAY QUEEN
1927.   TR. No 2.

BOOTLE MAY

MISS MARGARET POTTER.
BOOTLE MAY QUEEN 1932.
T.R.1.

Above: Four Queens smile from their carriage in North Park during the 1931 May Day. Left to right: Edna May Fairweather (May Queen), Bertha Prince (Dowager Queen), Jessie Greenwood (Gymnast Queen) and Phylis Spence (Railway Queen).

Left: Terence Ridgeway photographed May Queen, Miss Mary Potter, in the garden of her home in 1932. She looks lovely in her dress and highly embroidered train of sequins.

A young, smiling Miss Dorothy McEwan in 1933.
Notice her hair in ringlets. It seems that all May
Queens had to have ringlets.

Miss Margery Roscoe in 1934 snapped by
an unknown cameraman – possibly Terence
Ridgeway. This must be the second day of her
reign as she is wearing her crown.

Miss Winifred Dunne is pictured with her ladies-in-waiting, page boys, and crown and sword bearer, in 1935.

This procession moves along Merton Road during the 1935 May Day Demonstration. The horse and cart belonged to Bennetts Ltd, Liverpool.

One of the most popular groups taking part were the jazz bands. This one had over 100 performers in it and must have been a wonderful sight.

One of the 'best' Bootle jazz bands was the Laguna Revellers, was formed in 1937 as a breakaway from the Eureka jazz band. Their signature tune was *Lilly of Laguna*. Pictured in Litherland Road during coronation year, 1937. Front centre is Albert Brew (leader), on the back row, fourth right, is Edith Kelshaw, and on the centre row, sixth from left is Walter Raybould.

Miss Jean McKenzie poses for her official group photograph after she was crowned. The page boys were Len Upton and Derek Finney.

A high level view of the proceedings in North Park, during the 1939 May Day. Miss Jean McKenzie and Dowager Queen, Miss Nina Mills, are flanked by a 'Beefeaters' guard of honour. The following year, 1940, saw the last May Day for the duration of the Second World War. The May Queen in 1940 was Nina Mills.

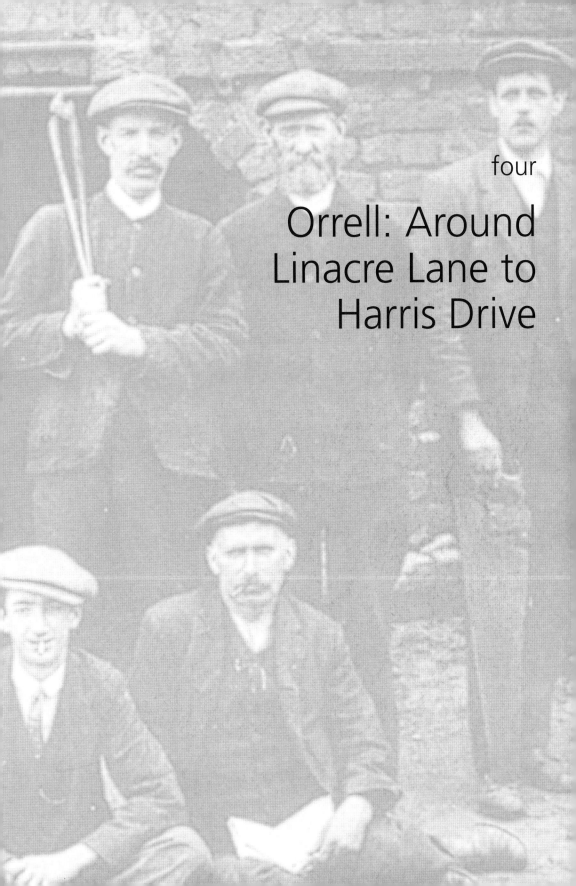

four

Orrell: Around Linacre Lane to Harris Drive

This postcard has been titled incorrectly by the photographer, it should read Stanley Road junction with Knowsley Road and Linacre Lane. To the left is Midland Bank, behind it is the Broadway Cinema. Behind the tram is St Andrew's church. On the right is Liverpool Savings Bank.

A corner view of Johnson Brothers, dyers and cleaners, Mildmay Road, in the 1990s. This part has been demolished and very soon the company will close for good. This lovely building has been the workplace for thousands of employees over a period of 100 years. It has also been a landmark on the Bootle skyline for all those years.

A reminder of Johnsons sports club. This is their hockey team in 1914 when they were Northwest Champions. Miss Christina Hayes, aged sixteen, is fourth from the right on the back row.

Some of the congregation of St Andrew's church, on a working party in September 1907. The postcard caption reads 'One volunteer is worth ten pressed men'. They are in the grounds of the church.

This 'Lifeboat Crew' are practising for either the Bootle May Day or the Litherland Gala, in 1910. They are pictured at the rear of St Andrew's church with their trainer.

Linacre gas works football team 1920/21 season. Their trainer was Tom Wilson of Patrick Avenue, pictured on the back row, far left. His son, also named Tom, is on the far right of the picture. The photographer was Percival Sutcliff of No. 457 Hawthorne Road, Bootle.

An ex-worker tearfully tends the grave of the passing of Linacre gas works in 1974. The headstone reads 'RIP Linacre Gas 1866-1974. Loved by some, mourned by many, served his country well'. The mourner is unknown.

Bootle Miniature Rifle Club held their meetings at the Linacre pub, Linacre Lane. Their shooting range was at the rear of the pub, against the canal wall. They are pictured with their Championship Shield which they won convincingly: fired 14, won 13, lost 1. Total points scored were 26.

St John's and St James' maintenance team is hard at work painting the railings around the church grounds. The original church was in a mission room in 1902, known locally as the 'tin mish'.

The foundation stone for this church was laid in 1910. Rising costs had made it impossible to maintain the upkeep of this beautiful church and it will unfortunately have to be demolished. It is not known when, but it will eventually come down. There are plans to build a modern single-storey building on the site, at the Monfa Road end. This is still in the planning stage, with no firm agreement as yet. These young men prepare to go on an outing.

This rare photograph is the only known pictorial record of No. 17 Province Road, Orrell. This was the home of Miss Rebecca Tennant, whose parents were the first tenants in Orrell, at 'Klondyke'. Rebecca was born in 1886 and died in 1986, in Connolly House, having just reached 100 years old. She is pictured chatting to the grandson of William 'Klondyke' Jones on her doorstep.

On the corner of Province Road and Hawthorne Road, which is the boundary of Bootle and Orrell, up high on the shop wall is a bit of local history. This is the only street sign with the name 'Orrell' on it. When these buildings come down with the rest of the 'Klondyke' this sign will be preserved, and possibly resited.

Left: W.R. White's at No. 8 Hawthorne Road, Bootle, baker and confectioner. The shop was also a sub-post office. Mr White is seen behind the window

Below: Willard Street, all decked out to celebrate the 1937 coronation. The children stand around excitedly waiting for the party to start. Despite rationing there were lots of jellies, cakes and butties to eat as well as lots of lemonade 'pop' to drink.

One of the best-loved shops on the 'Klondyke' was Spensley's sweets, tobacconists and toy shop. It was a haven for many a bus driver from the nearby bus garage, who would stop outside the shop and enjoy a welcome cuppa from Mrs Spensley.

Staley Street, was another street decorated for the 1937 coronation. Its main decoration was a very large crown, which does not look very safe. These streets seem wide here, being empty of motor vehicles, as well as being neat and clean.

On the site now occupied by the 'Mel-Inn' social club was part of the clay pits and kilns used in the construction of the 'Klondyke'. These men were some of the builders on the site. They worked for William Jones. They are believed to be Bob Evans, Dick Owen, Bob Roberts, Bill Ellis, Griff Williams (foreman) and ? Pritchard.

Hawthorne Road at its junction with Harris Drive. Looking back towards Staley Street, on the left are the sheds that were part of the 'Penpoll' Tin Smelting Company which moved from the site where the 'Mel-Inn' club stands to the opposite side of the road. The site was eventually sold to Campbell and Isherwood, whose offices are shown on the left.

Just off Harris Drive is Melville Road. These houses were built in 1935 by Willowbrook Estates. The street name was submitted on behalf of the builders. All the mums and kids pose for a group photograph prior to the Victory in Europe party in 1945.

Winner of the W.J. Terry Challenge Cup for bowls was Arthur Hughes, aged 47. The event in 1957 was held at Silcocks Sports Ground, Orrell Road, Orrell. As can be seen from the postcard he received the challenge cup (to be held for one year), a replica to keep and a canteen of cutlery.

Right: At Silcocks Sports Ground, Arthur H. Hughes (winner) shakes hands with the runner-up, Ben Stafford, after the bowls tournament in 1957. Although no longer connected with the Silcocks company, the ground still retains the name. St Robert Bellarmines is in the background.

Below: St Robert Bellarmine's church at the top of Orrell Road. The shops on the left occupy the site where Orrell Hey and Orrell Lodge once stood.

View of Orrell, *c.* 1898. The Orrell of today, over a century later, is quite different. In the right foreground now is Cinder Lane. In those days the streets would have been lined by the gateposts and railings of the large houses, including Orrell Lodge. Beyond the trees on the left was Day's farm on the corner of Park Lane.

OLD ENGLISH HALL FOR ORRELL.

A sketch of the proposed community buildings for Orrell designed to look like an 'old village hall'. Plans were put forward by Messrs Peter Walker & Sons, brewers, in 1930 but objections were raised by local people, churches and the family of William 'Klondyke' Jones. It was rejected by the council.

Right: Nina Owen, aged six years in 1938, stands on the front path of her home at 86A Park Lane, Orrell. Sixty-one years later she made a nostalgic trip from her home in America to Bootle and stood on the same spot as seen in this photograph.

Below: Tucked away behind Watts Lane and Park Lane is Roberts Drive School. In the season 1947/48 their junior football team was, from left to right, back row: ? Woodcock, H. Bradley, C. Stevens, D. Benyon, ? McVitie, G. Beattie. Front row: -?-, G. Adams, D. Watkins, J. Forbes, E. Bailey.

Other local titles published by Tempus

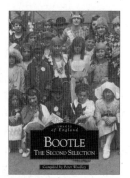

Bootle: The Second Selection
PETER WOOLLEY

This collection of over 230 old photographs of Bootle provides a nostalgic look back at this Merseyside community throughout the twentieth century. Many of the images show people going about their everyday business or partaking in all types of activities and events in Bootle over the years, while a section of the book illustrates the Bootle May Days.
07524 2454 8

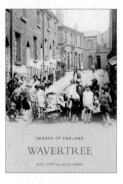

Wavertree
MIKE CHITTY & DAVID FARMER

Compiled by Mike Chitty and David Farmer on behalf of the Wavertree Society, this absorbing collection of old images trace some of the changes and developments that have taken place in Wavertee during the last 150 years. This collection of over 210 postcards and photographs highlights Wavertree's transformation from an agricultural village situated on the edge of Liverpool into a busy inner-suburban community.
07524 3068 8

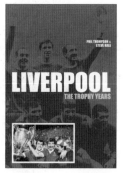

Liverpool The Trophy Years
PHIL THOMPSON & STEVE HALE

From the moment Bill Shankly arrived in 1959 and set about turning Liverpool Football Club into a world football force, trophies have found their way into the Anfield cabinet on a regular basis. From the Second Division Championship in 1894 and through the halcyon days of the 1960s to the remarkable treble of Worthington, FA and UEFA Cups in 2001 this book celebrates the triumphs and the players that achieved them.
07524 2951 5

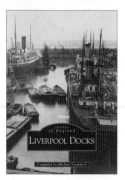

Liverpool Docks
MICHAEL STAMMERS

The story of Liverpool is, in many ways, the story of its docks. With contemporary illustrations of people, ships, buildings and machinery, Michael Stammers chronicles not just the rise and fall of Mersey shipping but also the way the docks have bounced back. Redevelopment, restoration and new modes of commerce have put Liverpool's docks back in the black, albeit looking very different to the port of sixty years ago.
07524 1712 6

If you are interested in purchasing other books published by Tempus, or in case you have difficulty finding any Tempus books in your local bookshop, you can also place orders directly through our website

www.tempus-publishing.com